HEAVEN REJOICES!

HEAVEN REJOICES!

Irene Park

Whitaker House

HEAVEN REJOICES

ISBN: 0-88368-434-9
Printed in the United States of America
Copyright © 1980 by Irene Arrington Park

Whitaker House
580 Pittsburgh Street
Springdale, PA 15144

2 3 4 5 6 7 8 9 10 11 12 / 06 05 04 03 02 01 00 99 98 97 96

Contents

Foreword

You are about to read a most remarkable testimony of God's grace. Irene Park is a gracious and gentle lady who radiates the peace of God. She loves Jesus with all of her heart and if you listen to her for even one minute, she will enthusiastically share with you her faith.

It is hard to imagine that Irene Park was once the High Wicked Witch of Florida; however, she was and according to her own testimony, she was the most wicked woman in America before being born again. The amazing grace of God has transformed a woman who offered blood sacrifices to obtain favors from the devil to be the strongest witch in all of Florida.

A drug dealer, pervert, smuggler, member of the underworld, worshipper of Satan and a blasphemer—Irene Park was these and more. Then Jesus Christ came. Powers of sin were broken.

As you read this remarkable book, you will be moved as I have been—sometimes revolted and sick at heart as you are confronted with the cruelty of the devil and the exceeding sinfulness of sin.

Please keep in mind that the sad and revolting story of Irene Park's early life must be told to have a new appreciation for the redeeming love of God. In no way should any reader of this book allow the devil to intimidate you or give you a spirit of fear. Rather, we should keep in mind that in the battle for Irene Park's soul, Satan lost. He was and is defeated and he will always be defeated by the living Christ.

So, read this shocking book and rejoice that the day of miracles is not past. Always remember—what God did for Irene Park, He will and can do for others.

No doubt you will want to share this book with a friend. Do not let the devil hinder. The Adversary must be recognized for the enemy that he is. Christ is the exalted hope for those bound by the slavery of sin.

H. Syvelle Phillips
Founder of Evangel Bible Translators

INTRODUCTION

Never before in history has our nation experienced such an onslaught of demonic activity—from "harmless" kid's games to open satanic worship. Towards this deluge, the Church, the Body of Christ, has largely remained silent in both real and feigned ignorance. It is not a nice, happy subject. But the Church for which Christ soon will return will have all things under its feet. To that end, this book is written.

In the book of Revelation, chapter 12, verse 12, John heard Heaven's prophecy, "Woe to the inhabitants of the earth and of the sea! For the devil is come down unto you, having great wrath, because he knoweth that he hath but a short time." Irene Park at the age of three fell prey to that wrath and in her own lust and deception for more than forty years freely yielded herself to every perversion and destruction of Satan, short of her own murder.

This book, though, is not primarily about Satan or his power. It is about the power, grace, mercy and love of God revealed through Jesus Christ and available to every believer through the power of prayer.

Irene's redemption and new life gives living testimony to the truth that, "Greater is He that is in thee than he that is in the world" (I John 4:4).

Jesus is still searching men's hearts to seek and to save them that are lost—from the most successful businessmen to those living in the depths of hell itself. When Jesus reached down to save Irene, the doctors said her body was beyond hope of healing, the psychiatrists said her mind was beyond hope of repair, and the government said her life was beyond hope of correcting. But our God specializes in the impossible and will save and deliver all who come to Him.

What makes Irene's present ministry so effective is not what she used to be but what Jesus has done for her--taken out her hard, stony heart and replaced it with a heart of love, restored her mind to rest free from lust, and miraculously renewed her body with healing and health.

Two and a half years ago I had the pleasure of performing the marriage ceremony of Irene to my dad. A beautiful, pure, new creation took my dad's hand that day and has since together shared in loving service to our King of Kings. Death is swallowed up in victory!

Pastor Jeffrey Park

"Know ye not that the unrighteous shall not inherit the kingdom of God? Be not deceived: neither fornicators, nor idolators, nor adulterers, nor effeminate, nor abusers of themselves with mankind.

Nor thieves, nor covetous, nor drunkards, nor revilers, nor extortioners, shall inherit the kingdom of God.

And such were some of you: but ye are washed, but ye are sanctified, but ye are justified in the name of the Lord Jesus and by the Spirit of our God."

I Corinthians 6:9-11

CHAPTER 1

PUSHING DOPE

"It seems so strange," I thought. The music was frantic—the electric guitars of The Grateful Dead were wailing to a discordant beat. Yet, everyone was loose and mellow. The whole crowd seemed totally oblivious to the violent electronic sounds of the concert right before them.

Business must be good tonight, I decided as I smelled the thick sweet aroma of marijuana which filled the Tampa stadium. My mind came alert—speaking of business, I'd better check on Don and Rickey. The urgency of checking on them heightened as my eyes caught sight of a policeman busting a young pusher not too far away from where I stood. I certainly didn't want any of my clan getting caught tonight. . . .

Selling marijuana, hash, cocaine and the pills, both uppers and downers, were our principal means of livelihood. And these big rock concerts always gave us a lot of business. But tonight there were too many pushers around so sales were certainly competitive. And the police knew it and were keeping a sharp eye out for any dealing going on.

If it wasn't for my spirit guide, Chief Red Horse, I would have been more nervous than I was—Satan's spirits would guide and protect us. But Don and Rickey worried me somewhat. They didn't seem to care much for things of the spirits; their heads were into the easy money and sexual freedoms they enjoyed.

By the time I found them, my fears were dispelled. They had already sold nearly all of their "wares" and were making friends with two young things, getting stoned and enjoying the show. They motioned for me to join them—I did and we partied on.

Back at the house I stepped into the kiva, the little room we had set up for our demon worship, and I knelt at the altar to give homage to Red Horse and the other demon spirits for protecting us through another night. "Avoiding the pigs is easy when the demons are with you," I thought.

Heading into the bedroom, I flirted with the idea of shooting up another fix of horse before hitting the sack. "Damn," I thought, "I wish we weren't out of cocaine." My body began to ache with pain and my mind was so exhausted. So I cooked up some junk, shot it up, and soon, once again, I was far, far away. . . .

The next week things were really getting to be a drag. We were without our best selling item, cocaine, and the local heat was really trying to put a stop to the heroin traffic so we had to be extra careful. This just made everyone uptight. My foster son, Pete, as well as Don and Rickey and even some of the girls had begun to fight among themselves.

Something had to be done. As the leader of the clan, I called a meeting of the disciples of Satan. As I let my spirit guide Red Horse speak through me, I told them that we had better let things cool off here. We were to take the clan West again to get a new supply of cocaine, marijuana and Mexican heroin to sell and return when the heat calmed down a bit.

As we headed West in Richard's van, my mind was invigorated. Although I was born right in South Florida, heading into Texas and New Mexico was for me, like heading back to my roots. For here I could go out to the mounds and chant and meditate with the spirits for hours until I could really feel the vibrations of the spirit world.

The spirits said it would be good to stay out of Florida for a while. So we settled down in a little town called Espanola near Santa Fe for a while. The men found work in a nearby meat plant and we put up some of the jewelry we'd stolen for rent on an apartment.

Because of some busts, we had to establish some new contacts for obtaining shipments out of Mexico. This was a hassle and caused us some delay—but it wasn't too long before we started thinking about pulling out. Since our money was low, the guys had to work a couple of more weeks and we had the girls selling sex and working con schemes to pick up enough money for the sale.

By the time we got the stuff, the guys were really uptight. I had to keep them from hanging Peter one night after he was out blowing coin. I convinced them to instead "tar and feather" him with butter and pillow feathers. It broke the tension, temporarily.

In the middle of waiting it out, my family in Florida got a message to me by way of the grapevine that one of my sisters had died. I felt like I wanted to scream and cry—but I couldn't. I felt a gnawing hurt deep within me but I couldn't express it. God knows I wanted to cry, but I couldn't!

I couldn't even tell the clan about it so I shot up some dope and went to bed. Both my body and my mind were exhausted and hurting.

"Mom, you're bleeding!" It was my daughter, Hope, back from school. She awakened me in a fright. Sometime during my sleep I had started to hemmorhage. I was too groggy to even answer her. Pete got Richard, Don, and the others and they tried to help me.

As my mind began to clear, I told Pete, "How could this be happening? It's been more than fifteen years ago since I had my hysterectomy?" With the help of a little food and more dope, I became oblivious to the physical pain. But I did know that the next two days were a living hell. . . .

When the last big shipment arrived, we had enough money at last so the men could turn in their resignations at work. We made our plans to return to Florida. I told the clan, "We'll leave tomorrow so we can be back in Florida while business is good for the Christmas holidays."

I was still weak so I had the guys carefully pack our belongings and load the van so we could head back to the southlands. All of us were tense and tired but excited about getting back to familiar territory once again.

When we arrived in Tampa, Pete convinced me to go to a doctor. He checked me out and said, "Lady, you are in one big mess. You need to get to a hospital and fast." When I flatly refused, the doctor agreed to try shots to coagulate my blood. He then told me to stay in bed for a week and if I didn't improve to get to the hospital without any more delay. I left his office, got a fix and went in to the fire gods to pray.

The clan was ecstatic. The stuff, especially the cocaine, we had brought back was of high quality and sales were brisk. I knew before we went West that a couple of us were being tailed by the heat, so we had to be careful.

Don and Rickey were to go and make a large delivery of amphetamines. As always, I sought the spirits for the direction they should take. We tried to never go and return the same route. They were given the instructions and everything seemed to be understood. But instead of coming back the route we had planned, they stopped at a friend's (my nephew's) house to party. Later, the three of them went to a drive-in for a snack. While waiting on the curb girls, they thought that a joint would sharpen their appetite, so they lit up. They were being far too careless; a police cruiser spotted them, radioed for additional help, and closed in and busted them.

I couldn't cry for Don or Rickey either. Actually, I didn't seem to even care. Bail was set. Since the friend was driving the car, the attorney said, he'd be the only one to get time if he would claim the drugs were his. We got the guys to make an agreement before the trial. After their release, we called some of our closest friends and satanic followers to join us for a party.

Since Don and Rickey had already been busted, we thought the heat was off. The police cruisers weren't buzzing the area as often so we were taking more chances.

The cocaine was already gone again so we partied on pot and heroin. That night some were in the bathroom cooking up some stuff for a fix. We had just finished when we heard a loud knock at the rear door. This door was used only by our pusher friends and close family.

Pete opened the door and unexpectedly in burst a troop of narcotic agents, badges flashing and revolvers drawn. The agent in charge barked orders, "We have a warrant to search this place. Everybody up against the wall, hands over your head and spread eagle."

Some of the agents started searching us and others started searching the rooms, particularly my son's and the attic. When they headed for the kiva, I protested, "You can't go in there. That's where we worship the spirits."

He answered as he kicked the door open, "Lady, you keep it shut. We'll do as we please." The only evidence they came out of the kiva with was some of the ceremonial corn we used in offerings to the fire god.

The agents had closed the entire area surrounding our house off to traffic during the raid. By the time they were through, the house was in shambles. We were all handcuffed and herded downtown.

There were nine of us to be processed, mugged and finger printed. Our clothes were taken and we were separated and given jail rags. Before being taken to my cell, I was allowed to make one call to the bondsman to come and get us out.

But he was slow. Waiting behind those cold steel bars was pure hell. The matron had been cold and crude. And the waiting was racking my nerves. The fix was wearing off and this was the last place in the world I wanted to be as I came down.

My eyes caught sight of a roach crawling between my feet. As I watched that foul-looking bug hunt around for food, I thought, "Where are my spirit guides now? What wrong turn had I taken to cause me to wind up caged in with a miserable roach for a companion?"

My mind went back to my childhood....

CHAPTER 2

LETTING THE DEVIL COME IN

It was mid-depression when I entered the world, specifically the world of Louie and Lettie Arrington, the sixth of nine children. Dad worked in a garage and did cabinet making and wood carving on the side. Mom worked in a canning plant to help make ends meet. Other than the fact that we kids had to do a lot of fending for ourselves, we were pretty much like other families in Western Florida during those times.

However, soon after my third birthday I was to experience a day of crisis that would steer my life off course for the next forty years. It was a hot summer day and, as usual, I was out playing in the backyard with my brothers and sisters. Inside the house we heard a great commotion—screaming, yelling and swearing. Then suddenly there were neighbors and strangers in the house.

Everyone was too busy or involved with the ruckus to explain what was happening to a little curly headed three year old. All I knew was that I wanted my daddy—and there he was. Just beyond the end of the walk, several policemen were tugging, pushing and hitting him.

"Daddy, Daddy. Stop hitting my daddy!" I screamed. "Help my daddy! Mommy, what are they doing?"

Even though I was only three, I was frantic. Daddy was practically my total world and now he was being dragged away by people whom I thought were Daddy's friends.

No one seemed to pay attention to my pleading or screaming except to hold me back from getting to Dad to help as they put him in the police car and drove away.

Rage filled my little heart. Oh, how I hated the men who took my daddy away! Our neighbors, the Browns, tried to calm me down by taking me over to their house. But I was hysterical.

"Help my daddy!" I cried. "Why won't anybody help get Daddy back?"

So Mr. Brown had to half drag me across the lawn—with me screaming and biting and kicking all the way. Mr. Brown was saying, "Irene, they are helping your daddy. He's had a nervous breakdown but he's going to be all right. You just take it easy and your daddy will be home soon."

My young mind couldn't understand about the nervous breakdown and somehow I didn't believe Dad would come back unless someone helped him away from those bad policemen. I was angry and determined to do something.

Mom had her hands full with all the kids, especially the baby, so she never did explain much to us. For days I went all around the neighborhood looking for Daddy.

A couple of days later my brothers and I were playing with the old water pump in the backyard and I said to them, "I'm going to run away and find Daddy."

Louie, who was just a year older, replied, "Irene, don't go until I'm old enough to go, too."

"I'm going now if I have to go by myself," I pouted. And climbed up into the huge bamboo bush to cry.

Suddenly, I heard a voice saying, "What is wrong?"

It wasn't my brothers. It was a tall, lean Indian standing in front of me. First, I just stared at him and then finally I said to him, "Those bad policemen have taken away my daddy and I don't know where he is."

Without a word, his eyes seemed to say, "Come with me and I'll take you to him." I jumped down out of the bamboo bush and began to follow him. Before long, I was walking uptown and climbing a big oak tree across from the police station where my daddy was being held. I couldn't see him but I was sure he was there.

Before long, a couple of policemen came near and I spit at them and shouted the worst words I could think of. One of the policemen recognized me and first tried to coax me down. When that didn't work, he left to call my mother.

I couldn't understand why the policemen didn't say anything to my Indian friend up in the tree. But when they left, the Indian began to lead me back home.

"What is your name?" I asked looking up at his cold but handsome appearance.

"My name is Chief Red Horse," he said.

When we got home, Mom was furious. I tried to explain to her what had happened, but she didn't believe me, especially the part about Chief Red Horse.

I said, "Chief Red Horse, tell Mom how you led me uptown." But then he was gone—vanished into thin air. And Mom said she never saw him though he was standing right next to me. "Your mind is just making that up and I'll not put up with that or that ugly talk to the policeman. Now get me a switch for your bottom," she ordered.

Only after I had gotten my whipping did Chief Red Horse appear again. "Maybe other people can't see him," I thought, "but he is going to be my best friend." And indeed that is what he became to me. He was always there to share my feelings with and we spent hours and hours together in the big bamboo bush.

This imaginary friend (who was really a familiar spirit) actually encouraged my anger, bitterness and rebellion. So with little parental care or discipline I was quickly developing a heart filled and controlled by Satan.

Dad remained in the hospital for several months and when he was released, he stayed at home only long enough to put together a truck which would hold him and his wood carvings. He had decided to travel the country exhibiting his art. I would crawl up on his lap and ask, "Where are you going, Daddy?" And he would reply, "Over all the world and half of Georgia."

Dad's interest in traveling was spurned on by his friendship with a clan of gypsies. And it was through these gypsies that I was first introduced to the occult. Ollie, a large black woman, gypsy, and palm reader, frequently babysat for us when Mom and Dad went out. Ollie practiced voodoo magic and all my brothers and sisters despised her because she was strange. But I found her interesting and as Ollie befriended me, I learned much from her about the world of spirits.

Though Ollie was neither pretty nor smart, she nearly always got her way. She had a strange dominance over people that was at first eerie to me. I came to learn this dominance came from her fearful power in the spirit world.

Ollie taught me how to put hexes on people she didn't like. She would take a chicken, cut its head off, and mix it with frog's intestines. Then she would take them and place them on the intended victim's doorstep. The putrid sight and smell was about enough to drive a person crazy. And I saw Ollie's potions literally do that to more than one person who crossed her will.

One of Ollie's favorite things to do was to go out to the cemetery late at night and call up dead spirits. I was afraid to go with her and while I didn't want to go, I wanted to act big, so I went along.

In the cemetery, Ollie would take a mixture of flour and oil and rub it on herself and then begin to wail and dance herself into a trance. Suddenly, I could feel the weird presence of evil spirits. I wanted to run like crazy but couldn't. I just stood shaking with fear until Ollie came to herself again.

I never understood why Ollie would do that. And when I told my little friends in the neighborhood what had happened, they wouldn't believe me. So I took two of them out to the cemetery myself to prove that I wasn't afraid.

Because of these graveyard visits, my friendship with Ollie and my attraction to an older girl who was a lesbian, my brothers and sisters began to call me "Crazy Irene." This hurt me deeply and further alienated me from my physical surroundings, intensifying my interest in Chief Red Horse, my "spirit friend." He was always friendly and would help me in almost anything. Whatever I would want, he would help me to get or find—like Dad's bootleg whiskey or his, or someone else's, cigarettes. At the age of eleven, I was smoking regularly and well on my way to becoming an alcoholic.

During this period of my childhood, my adventure into the spirit world took on a new dimension. At certain seasons, the Seminole Indians would come up from their reservation in the Florida Everglades. They would camp on the grounds at the Singing Tower in nearby Lake Wales.

Dad, being part Indian, had once taken us over to visit. But soon I was going over to their campgrounds by myself. There I met Joe Billy, an Indian lad just a couple of years older than me.

We became close companions. I would tell Joe Billy about the friends I had that no one else could hear or see. Though he couldn't see Chief Red Horse, he seemed to understand. "Irene," he said, "our people talk to the spirits all the time. There is a great respect for the wisdom of the spirits and the medicinemen of the Seminoles."

Joe Billy explained to me how the Indians lived and taught me much about their history and culture. So a strong bond grew between us during the times that the Seminoles came to the Tower.

Mom neither liked nor understood my friendship with the Indians and tried to keep me from seeing them with bamboo whippings. But even this did not stop me.

My relationship with my spirit friends (Chief Red Horse introduced me to others) was also growing and became a compelling force within me. It got such that I could hardly go into a store; for when I did, I would steal something. Mom would usually return the item and make me give an apology to the store manager.

My strange and evil habits were nearly driving the family crazy. Mom was a religious (Southern Baptist) person and did all she could to teach us right from wrong. When I was about ten, Daddy left for good with his gypsy friends. So Mom had to be both Mother and Father to all nine of us.

We bathed once a week on Saturday nights to look our best for Sunday church. I didn't mind going to church because as soon as the singing was over I would sneak out. Outside the church my brothers and I would scavenge the long cigarette butts of those who would have a quick smoke between Sunday School and church. We would then divide our "finds" and smoke them.

When I was fourteen, Ann, one of my married sisters, moved to Tampa and suggested to Mom that if I would come live with her, it might help straighten me out. Mom had already tried sending me to a psychiatrist and that hadn't helped any. And now she was plain exhausted. That year she had spent almost as much time at school as I did because I was forever forgetting to go. . . .

Therefore, Mom consented to my going to live with Ann and her husband. And for a few days, it seemed that I was really going to be a different person. But as I got bored, I began to talk to my spirit guide, Red Horse. He told me where my brother-in-law kept his smokes hid and I was right back to my old tricks again. Since my sister was busy with her new baby, there was plenty of time for me to explore my new surroundings and make new friends—including those in the spirit world.

CHAPTER 3

THE SEDUCING SPIRITS

Without discipline or direction, my life at Ann's gravitated to the path of least resistance, which was usually doing that which was wrong or evil. In the neighborhood, I became friends with Marsha, a girl who was my age—and gay. For kicks, Marsha and I decided to run away together.

Neither of us had more than a couple of dollars so we didn't get very far. We wound up only across town at the Royal American Carnival Show. Bill, a chubby old cigar-smoking Italian, gave us jobs working in the concession stands. Quickly, Marsha and I learned the art of conning and all the other schemes of carnival life. Bill didn't care how much money we made as long as he got his share of the take. Marsha and I kept half of what we took in and stored it in our shoes.

Out of curiosity, I began to venture up and down the midway, taking in the shows with the freaks and illusions, the palm readers, crystal ball gazers and the fortune tellers. Some of the show operators, of course, were outright frauds but others, particularly those run by the gypsies, genuinely believed in the satanic, psychic practices they performed. These people had a beguiling and seducing influence on me.

From our old babysitter, Ollie, I had discovered that it was possible, by the spirits, to mentally control people. But these gypsies had such manipulatory powers that it was frightening. Oddly, at the same time, the evil spirits in me bore witness to them and caused me to want to befriend them. Before long, I was the "little darling" of the midway.

Bill knew that both Marsha and I were under age. But he let us sleep right in the concession stand where we worked. "Just don't get caught," he growled. After a couple of nights, Freddy, who also worked the concessions and was a homosexual, invited us to sleep in his room until we earned (and stole) enough money to get our own room. Only the glitter and intrigue of carnival life hid the loneliness of being fourteen and separated from all my family.

One afternoon, Freddy ran over to our concession booth and said, "There have been a couple of city vice detectives over at my stand, asking about you two. They were flashing your photographs and quizzing me where they might find you." Fortunately, there is an unwritten law among carnies to "never tell the police anything about anyone." So Freddy protected us for the moment.

Not far from the carnival grounds, there was a quaint little bar that gave free horse and buggy rides to its patrons. Marsha and I had gone there occasionally and we decided that we could best "lie low" by losing ourselves in the crowd on the buggies. The buggy in which we were riding had just about returned to the bar when I heard someone yelling.

Instantly, I recognized the voice as that of an Arrington. It was my little brother calling, "Hey, that's my sister, Irene! Hey, Irene! Irene!"

I waved back to him and yelled, "Go back! Please go back! I can't come with you now but I'll see you later." Oh, how I wanted to tell him how much I loved them and missed them all, but I couldn't. He kept running after our buggy until we were out of sight.

My brother's seeing me was sure to mean problems, especially since the detectives were alerted to my disappearance. Sure enough, the police were contacted and there was a cruiser at the bar waiting for me. This began the frequent trips I would take to the inside of a jail.

One day someone at the jail suggested that I get married "to a man." They told me, "If you get married, your family can't have you put away anymore." It sounded like a good idea so I set out to find a husband. This was not a big problem for an experienced con artist as myself and in just a few weeks, Tony, a young tough, two years my senior, proposed to me in the back seat of his souped up old Chevy.

After we found a justice of the peace and paid our five dollar marriage fee, home to Mama I went, showing off my new husband. She was too tired of me to either protest or act pleased.

I knew nothing about love and I looked at Tony mostly as my means of escaping the hassles with the police. As a result, I was a horrible wife. I continued my gay relationship with Marsha and my friendship with the other gypsies. I was rarely home and gave my husband no more attention than a child would give an old doll.

Actually, Tony was a fairly nice guy and at times I wanted to be a wife and settle down; but then a passion would come over me and I could change like Jekyll and Hyde. There were unsatiable driving desires within that I couldn't control. The further I travelled down the dark evil path of sin, immorality and corruption, the firmer the grip these passions had on my life. Alcohol, illicit sex, marijuana (or "locoweed" as Joe Billy, my young Indian friend, had called it), and occultism of every form held my attention.

Then there were times that I would try hard to live

a normal life. I had never really lived around the kind of people to know what a normal life was, but I tried to learn from my neighbors and the couple of married sisters with whom I had contact. Tony was patient and helpful, thinking that I just had a wild spirit that needed taming. He tried new places and new activities for us, but my old evil ways always tugged me back.

Soon Tony gave up and tired of our arrangement. For the time being, he had provided me freedom from the police, so I gave him his freedom. I thought, "I have Red Horse, my life-long companion. Who needs a man?"

Several years later I married husband number two and he and I adopted two small but beautiful Indian children, Richard and Hope. This marriage, like the first, and the third, all ended in divorce. The third man was nearly as perverted as I. Paul was an alcoholic and got his kicks out of sex orgies and wild partying. Invariably, I would become jealous and start a fracas, which always meant one of us would leave or the police would have to come and break us up. These bouts would leave me exhausted and confused.

Feeling terribly alone, I attempted suicide several times. One day in a state of utter frustration, I called Alcoholics Anonymous. Something had to happen because I just couldn't put up with this melee any longer. I was desperate, wanting this perverted man and his friends out of my life and out of our home. The people in the AA program were very understanding. The "kindred spirits" in the program were clearly the finest people I had ever met.

About the same time, my problem with Paul resolved itself, temporarily. One weekend, he got involved in a sex orgy on a boat docked in the Tampa Bay. When it sailed, he went along on to the Caribbean and that was the last that I saw of Paul for months.

But dealing with my own problems wasn't easy. I hadn't realized what a terrible alcohol addiction I had until I tried to quit. In the morning, I'd be lonely and ease the pain with a drink. By afternoon, I'd feel restless; that would mean more drinking and, at night, I'd drink just to go along with the crowd. I was trying hard to fight this desire when my AA sponsor, Francis, a beautiful woman of God, saw me crying at a meeting.

She came and put her arms around my neck. "Irene," she said, "It can't be all that bad. Do you want to tell me about it?"

"It's no use," I cried. "I've really tried to stop drinking but I'm only getting worse. Those things inside me won't let me go."

Tenderly, she took hold of my hand and said, "I understand what you are saying and I know someone who can help you. Now I want you to promise me that you won't do anything or go anywhere until I can arrange for you to see them."

She was so sweet, I really didn't believe that she understood my problem, but I didn't have anywhere else to go, so I agreed. "O.K., but please help me soon," I said.

The next day Fran took me to the Christian Medical Foundation. There I met two women, Martha Lazarus and Kay Reed, wife of the Director. Almost instantly, I recognized that these women had something that I wanted; they were so peaceful. There was none of the frenzy that characterized my gypsy friends. They even looked different and smelled fresh and clean.

Kay began talking to me about the Lord Jesus Christ. She shared, "Irene, Jesus is bigger than any problem you have. He can be just as real in your life as He has been in mine. You know He has helped me through every difficulty that I've ever had. Whenever I have a problem or need, He's always there to help."

"And, Irene, Jesus doesn't just help the so-called good people. He came to save us sinners. Jesus loves you regardless of what you've been and He will forgive you for every sin that you've committed."

She knelt with me and I asked the Lord to come into my heart. It was like a spark of light had pierced through the darkness of my soul. For the first time in my life, I began to feel really happy and alive!

CHAPTER 4

AN ATTEMPT AT A NEW LIFE

As the first days of my new life passed, I hardly noticed the changes going on around me. But inside, something was happening. My desires were different. For the first time in my life, I became interested, even excited, about the Bible. Whether reading alone or with the children, I couldn't get enough of God's Word or prayer. We were invited to several prayer circles and began to attend regularly. At the first prayer meeting, I told my friend Fran, "All of this is very familiar because it's almost identical to the way the spiritualists and Satanist worship. The big difference is the presence of love through Jesus Christ."

My old friends came by less and less, and eventually quit coming altogether. I even stopped seeing my gypsy brothers and sisters. Hope and Richard attended church with me and, before long, they, too, had accepted Christ as their Savior. The peace and harmony that Christ brought to our home was wonderful.

But then several months later, the inevitable happened. I was home cooking supper one evening when the phone rang. It was my husband, Paul. He began, "Irene, honey. I love you and miss you. I want to come home. Is it all right if I come back?" "Oh, no," I thought—just when I'd been praying that God would keep him away. I wanted to tell him to go get lost but he persisted that things would be different this time. Finally, I said, "Paul, I've become a Christian and I need to talk with some of my Christian friends about this before I give you an answer."

This was the truth and as soon as Paul hung up, I called Sister Carmen Vazquez, one of the mature Christians in our prayer group. "Carmen," I cried, "that lousy Paul just called and wants to come back. He's no good and I hate him; now what do I do?"

"Hold on, Irene!" she said calmly. "Now you don't hate anybody. The Lord will work things out. All you have to do is trust Him."

Carmen was wrong. I did hate Paul. The hatred that I had felt at the age of three toward those that took my dad away was now directed toward my husband. I had never truly forgiven him and gotten cleansed of this evil within me.

At a further meeting with Carmen, instead of dealing with this, she told me, "It is God's will that you be with your husband. Let him come home. God can change his heart." I didn't have faith that this would happen but I agreed out of pure obedience. At first, it appeared that Carmen was right. Paul was considerate and seemed happy with the changes in the home and in me. But things went downhill fast. It started when I said, "no" to his suggestions of perverted sex. Then I told him, "There will be no more witchcraft in this house and no more orgies with your old friends."

Paul stormed out of the house and returned hours later, very drunk and foulmouthed, determined to make a wreck out of me. And he largely succeeded. Our increasingly frequent fights upset the children and neighbors until once again the police were called in to referee our violent quarrels.

In front of others, including my Christian friends,

Paul would appear kind and pretend as though everything was great between us. This was a lie. Hatred and
anger were boiling inside of me and now it appeared
that even my Christian friends had turned against me,
wanting me to put up with this miserable hell. I couldn't
take it any longer. Instead of going to my pastor or talking out this problem with God in prayer, I began talking
to myself.

Soon I was hearing that familiar voice; it was Red
Horse. Then there were more voices and I started re-
lating to what they were telling me. For they were sym-
pathetic to my hatred for Paul and encouraged my
feelings of bitterness and resentment until I really
wanted to kill him.

Finally, I went to an attorney and he suggested we
get a divorce. I knew this was against the wishes of my
Christian friends so I felt guilty to be around them.
Over the next several months, I began to lose hope in
God and gradually stopped attending church and the
prayer meetings.

Pretty soon I was doing the same things as before I
got saved. My zest for life and the things of God fizzled
out from lack of fellowship and prayer. Normal things
in life again became a bore and I was now back in the
trap of Satan and his stronghold....

CHAPTER 5

TOTAL DARKNESS IN SATAN'S KINGDOM

Having lost my joy in Christ, I began smoking marijuana openly. One iniquity leads to another, and soon I was holding seances, readings, casting spells, placing hexes and making fetishes. I sold out to Satan completely and his rewards were enticing. All kinds of people recognized me as a leader and advisor and came to sit under my teaching in the realm of the occult. I enjoyed the feeling of power, even if it was demonic.

Richard and Hope, now teenagers, followed me back into drugs and the occult and before long another half a dozen young people including Peter, a foster son, joined our "family," accepting my authority and leadership. My sensitivity to the vibrations of the spirit world returned and grew. In performing sorcery and conjuring up spirits from Satan's realm, I found powers of darkness like I had never experienced before. Submitting myself totally, I became tuned in to the highest vibrations and experienced the supernatural continually.

But most of all, I was enjoying the power of being the leader of the clan. I knew all this was wrong, but I rationalized my conscience away by saying, "I'm using these powers for good. After all, aren't people receiving supernatural guidance and some even being healed?"

The instance I was referring to involved Mike, one of the new young men in our clan. He had learned that his grandfather in Tallahassee was dying of a heart attack and members of his family were in town to take him home. When Mike shared this with me, I went in and offered sacrifices before the spirits that they might relax their grip of death on this man. They did and Mike's grandfather got well temporarily—at the expense of more of Mike's family being seduced into witchcraft.

Soon smoking marijuana was neither enough to get me high nor to drown out my conscience, even when I mixed smoking with alcohol. Conveniently, Tim, a guru who had come to learn about the occult, was also a large drug dealer. He was in the living room snorting some cocaine one afternoon when I came in. I asked, "How about sharing some of that white stuff with me?"

He smiled, "Why sure, pretty mama! This is a trip; you're going to go for a good ride." I began snorting cocaine regularly and before long was shooting up heroin. There was no way that I could support the kind of habit I was building, even at Tim's discount prices.

Through some higher contacts in organized crime, Tim was getting in huge shipments of drugs by boat from South America and by plane from Old Mexico. He invited our clan to assist for a price in the distribution. We began pushing marijuana and hard core drugs and fencing stolen merchandise for some of Tim's friends.

When Tim's contacts recognized our "cooperation," it wasn't long before we were pushing pornography and sex for hire. We had connections for every kind of filth, corrupt, and illegal deals, even on an international scale. There was no end to the avenues of crime and violence our family stooped to.

I became openly satanic. Soon I was even offering up blood sacrifices to the demonic powers that were controlling me. I even forced my own son Richard and nephew Don to submit to the knife in drawing blood for these sacrifices. Often I told myself that one day I would stop this, but instead, there came an unquenchable passion for power and more power. I remembered the Indian burial mounds that I had visited with my young Indian friend in Lake Wales years before—how we had spent time meditating and how strong spiritually I had felt after going to the burial grounds. So I began making plans for a new vigil to the Indian mounds, but this time out West.

Our "family" had by this time gotten so deeply involved in hard core drug distribution that we all couldn't just leave. So Tim agreed to stay behind. But the rest of us piled into Richard's new van (our criminal activity had become quite profitable) and headed toward New Mexico and Indian country.

I wasn't exactly sure where we would wind up once we got out West, but I was confident that Red Horse and the others would show me. And sure enough, as we were passing through some Tewa country (a tribe of the Pueblos) along the higher plateaus near Santa Fe, the spirits said, "This is it. You are to stay here for awhile."

We found the Tewa Indians friendly and open to allowing us to camp in an arroyo (ravine) at one end of their reservation.

After checking out the area and establishing a friendly repoire with the tribal leaders, I immediately sought out the place of the Indian burial mounds.

"This is surely the leading of the spirits," I thought. Their mounds were very similar to the ones that I had been around and laid on years earlier. But this time, I had come for an entirely different reason and I didn't intend to leave empty-handed. I began walking the arroyo, chanting and praying. After dusk I sat on some rocks and began chanting and singing in the Indian language. It wasn't long before I could feel the presence of the spirits of the dead; then we were all chanting and dancing.

My previous experiences with Indian ritual had taught me that you could please the spirits with ceremonial corn. I put out some ceremonial corn that I had brought for the spirits to eat and I ate some myself. Red Horse, my Spiritual Guide, told me there needed to be a blood sacrifice, how to do it, what the sacrifice was for, and what would happen during the sacrifice. Shortly after this, among the mounds, I came across a very hard black stone. When I rubbed this stone, strange vibrations went through my body. I seemed to be leaving my body and felt myself floating and losing attachment with the natural. I realized later I had been in a trance and the powers of evil were using me. At the time, I thought I was using them and still was in control, but I had already largely given up my soul to the devil.

CHAPTER 6

MYSTERIOUS WORSHIP AND WITCHCRAFT

As we dwelt there in the village with the Tewa Indians, I became more and more intrigued with their rituals and order of life. Partly because of my Indian blood on my father's side and partly because of my sensitivity to the spirits (of the dead), I became freely accepted in the tribe almost as if I were one of them.

What I experienced with the Tewas is not necessarily similar to the tribal rituals of other Indian tribes and it is not shared to judge or condemn their way of life. It is, however, the reality of my experience and it illustrates the need for evangelism and the ministry of the Holy Spirit to a great populace of people in this country who have been largely ignored by the Christian community. One reason that evangelism has not been very successful among the Indians is that Holy Spirit empowered deliverance is needed for the many caught in the web of satanic ritual practices.

In the Tewa village, I found that much of their life was centered around the medicine men, superstitions, idolatry, ritualism, spiritual dances and sacrifices and various forms of spiritualism. The whole order of government and leadership of the tribe draws every man, woman and child into its web. The medicine men are held in highest respect and they pass the traditions and superstitions down from generation to generation.

Just as we teach our children American history and take them to Sunday School to learn of God, the Indians take their children (especially the young boys) to the medicine men to learn the Indian heritage and ritualism and how to please the spirits of the tribe.

The boys and young men are taken to learn in the kiva, the room or area where the secret ceremonials, prayers and tribal rituals are held. In our village, the kiva was a round adobe (mud and straw) structure, centrally located in the village plaza. Stairs led up to the entrance and down into the interior. On the walls inside were Indian signs, images, idols and gods of human, fowl and beastly elements.

The medicine men explain the meaning of the signs and teach the boys how to chant. As they mature, they are brought into more strict discipline and deeper secrets. As I observed the youth, I was impressed with the seriousness and sincerity in which they underwent their training (much unlike the free spirited American youth). Their intensity showed that they greatly desired the power that comes with obedience to the medicine men. The respect of these leaders held by the youth is awesome. The young girls undergo similar training from the older women but it is not as much spiritually oriented.

The medicine men award obedience and sincerity by pronouncing names of animals or fowl upon the young at various stages of their training. As the young men advance, they must spend longer periods in the kiva alone, fasting, meditating and communing with the spirits. Gradually, they are brought into the village ceremonials with the men. This is a highlight and honor for any youth.

When a ceremonial is to begin, the drummers and chanters gather at dusk around the outside of the kiva, bringing just the right vibrations so the spirits (demons) can work. Ahead of time the medicine man has gathered the piyote buttons which will be smoked or chewed. He has also prepared a potent beverage brewed from the piyote roots and other plants. By using these drugs in the ceremony, the mind is made pliable to the supernatural powers of Satan and his angels.

Usually women are allowed in the ceremonials only to carry in and out food. But on several occasions I was allowed to observe the ceremonies from inside the kiva.

When the men are seated in the kiva and partake of the piyote, usually the older men begin singing (actually more like talking) in a rhythm of stories and chants of the past. As the singing and chanting becomes intensified, a person will be transformed, taking on the expression of a fowl or beast. Sometimes this will be further exhibited in dancing as the demons take control.

More than once, I saw such a powerful demonstration of the spirits during a ceremonial that a young brave would back out of the kiva in fear. To do this, though, is to lose face in the sight of the tribe. Rather, it is regarded an honor when the spirits choose to manifest themselves through you. The costumes of hides and antlers and feathers used in the ceremonies all are appeals to please the spirits.

At different times of the year, different ceremonials are held to please and honor the different spirits that were regarded as ruler over the rain, sun, crops, hunting, etc. And even in the Indian homes, there was always a secret ceremonial place where the spirits were honored and worshipped. Images of animals, fowl, sun, moon, or stars, carved from stone, bone or wood would be placed behind a bowl where the ceremonial corn would be placed. This was their altar.

In the village where I was, there had been some Roman Catholic influence in the past so some of the Indians had replaced their animal images with images of a saint or even Jesus. It was still mostly idolatry.

Because of the language barrier, I didn't understand all that was being said in the ceremonials. But Red Horse and the other spirits with whom I was sharing would explain to me much of the meaning. As I lived with the Indians and learned their heritage, traditions and rituals, a surge of power and excitement filled me. As I observed these things, the spirits told me that they would be with me and help me to also lead a mighty tribe. I believed these spirits and by the time I headed back to Florida with my growing clan to continue our life of crime, drugs and lust, I had evidence to substantiate what they were saying was true.

There was clarity in my spiritual communication with the spirits; I was exercising complete mental control over my clan and there were those who came and asked to join our clan because they could recognize the power that I exerted.

If I knew that lying ahead in Florida was a few months of partying, another trip West, and then only illness, jail and hassles, I would have stayed with the Tewas.

CHAPTER 7

THE TURNING OF THE WORM

As I sat on the hard jail bunk in Tampa, waiting for the bondsman, I thought, "Am I really being messed around in a web of treachery or had my spirit guide just made a mistake? But then, really there wasn't much choice left now anyway. I had tried to live differently and couldn't, so I would just have to try to make the best of the road I had taken." Finally, here was the bondsman and I could say "goodbye" to the bars and the roaches.

As soon as we were released, I stopped by a friends's house for some drugs. By the time I got home and shot up, I was really hurting and shaking. I knew that my authority and leadership of the clan was now threatened because of the bust and I would have to pull myself together. Richard and Tim were already asking, "What do we do now?" And I didn't have any answers.

Going into the kiva, I offered up some ceremonial corn and tried to get still to attune myself to the spirits. But my mind was going in too many directions to hear much.

There was a knock at the door. It was Tim (he had moved out of the house but was still part of the clan) with his girlfriend, Gail. Tim could see I was unnerved.

He grabbed me and bit my neck, "Don't worry, Mama. No sweat, everything is still cool. Here, I brought you some good weed and some pills. Let's just relax and have a little party."

It broke the tension, and pretty soon others had come and joined in and we all partied as if nothing had happened. But when the outsiders had left, I called the clan together to discuss our situation. I began, "This bust was not the fault of our spirit guides. If Don and Richey had obeyed instructions, the heat would have never come down on us in the first place. We've just been plain too damn careless!

"Just think, if the narcs had raided us tomorrow evening instead of tonight (a large shipment of heroin and pills was scheduled to arrive the next day), we'd all still be frying in the joint. So, actually, we were really lucky; with the few pills and works that they found tonight, they probably can't make a case against any one of us. But we've gotta be more careful. You guys are going to have to get regular jobs for awhile and we'll have to keep our action at a minimum."

They all reluctantly agreed and seemed satisfied with my handling of the whole affair. This was a great relief because inside I was as shakey as a leaf.

Over the next few weeks, I continued giving sittings, holding seances, and giving psychic readings to other people, but inside my life was rapidly falling apart with one disaster after another. The nephew that was out on bond for possession of amphetamines pulled an armed robbery, was caught and jailed without bond. And my body was going from bad to worse. Regardless of what or how much drugs I shot up, it didn't stop the pain.

But worse of all, it was the same way with the spirits. I couldn't seem to communicate with them anymore. I would go into the kiva, sit on the floor and meditate for hours. Even rubbing the polished stones, placing the feathers around the altar, offering the ceremonial corn, and lighting the incense was bringing no response. "There had to be a reason for this," I thought.

Finally, I cried out in torment one night, "Come on, damn you, spirits. What's the matter? Has hell gone on strike? I know you're out there; why won't you come to me?"

Still no response. I began to chant and pray softly, "Red Horse, you've been with me for so long. If I've offended you, just let me know. What do you want from me anyway? Do you want blood?"

And finally there came an answer. It was short and clear. "Yes, blood."

Bewildered, tired, confused and feeling never so alone in the spirit world, I wasn't sure I could get the sacrifice together. I decided to try to calm down first with some dope. One of the guys in the house had some dilaudid and agreed to split it with me. He cooked up the fix, tied off my arm and drove the needle into the vein.

"Oh, God! Oh, I'm dying," I cried. The stuff must have been poison, for as soon as it hit my bloodstream, I became violently ill, shaking like someone having an epileptic seizure and upchucking as I had never done before. My whole body went into convulsions and my mind was spinning like a top out of control.

Walter, the guy who'd given me the bad stuff, and Richard managed to carry me over to the bed and hold me down until I passed out from exhaustion. I came to the next morning and called the whole clan together for a meeting later that day.

I told Richard, "If the spirits want blood, that's exactly what we'll give them." Richard thought I meant an animal sacrifice and went out to prepare it. Actually, I wasn't sure what I meant, but if there was betrayal in our clan, I was planning on stopping it today—even if it meant offering up a human sacrifice. And in preparation of that, I arranged several knives under some articles near the altar.

When the clan had gathered in a circle, I spoke, "Something is wrong! The spirits have rejected my worship lately and today we're going to find out why. Before we pray, we will pass the cup (chalis containing the blood of an animal) and you will attest your loyalty and devotion to Satan."

There was one girl in the circle that had given me bad vibes all along and I was certain the passing of the cup would "make or break" her. As I passed the cup to each one, fixing my gaze steadfastly on each as they partook of the sacrifice, I noticed she was becoming tense and nervous.

When I got to her and placed the cup in her hands, I asked, "Tricia, is something bothering you?" Without answering, she took the cup and sipped and passed it back to me and shook her head.

"She's passed the test," I thought. "Surely the spirits would have shown me if she was lying." But as it turned out, Tricia was lying, for we learned later that she was a police informer. But by God's grace, He spared her life that day—and ours, too, because in our warped state, we could easily have killed her.

Thank God that He loves us and protects us when we are His enemies—even one who was sold out to the devil.

CHAPTER 8

IRENE, JESUS LOVES YOU

Since the drug bust at the house, both our dealing and using drugs there had to be confined to a minimum. So with Christmas coming up, we made plans for a big party at a house out on the river. It was going to be the biggest blast of the year.

The grounds were decorated with colorful lights; tents and pads with sleeping bags were conveniently arranged; barbeque grills were brought in; rock music blasted from every direction; and kegs of beer and b.y.o.d. (bring your own drugs) made the party complete. I had reserved my special place on the patio. Lying completely naked on a lounge chair, I was going to serve as "queen of the orgy."

My exposure started something and soon most everyone was partying together—totally in the nude. The whole scene became a maize of evil and demonic delight; when suddenly Peter came running up on the patio, yelling, "Mom, get on some clothes, quick! Cover yourself with anything! Mrs. Tatum and some other lady are coming up the lawn."

I couldn't believe it. Mrs. Tatum was a friend of the family and a dedicated Christian. I had not seen her in over three years.

"Tim, hand me my robe, quick," I hollered. And before I could get "buttoned up," around the corner of the house came Mrs. Tatum and her friend.

I was too shocked at their audacity to barge in on our party to even say hello. I was even more shocked at the way they were acting as if nothing was going on. Kindly, Mrs. Tatum spoke first, "Hello, Irene. It is so good to see you again."

Meanwhile, Mrs. Tatum's friend, Inez, stopped to chat with some of the clan. When she had found Hope, she put her arm around her and together they made their way toward me.

I was disgusted and confused. "What the hell do you think you're doing, busting in on us like this?" I scowled. This wasn't the first time some of my old Christian friends had tried to reach me.

Katherine wasn't intimidated and, releasing Hope's hand, she moved over to my chair. Smiling, she said softly, "Irene, Jesus Christ died for you, just for you. He loves you and He will always love you. We know what is going on here and we know God is going to help you, Irene. He is going to save you and all of these children."

I was numb. "Tatum," I cried, "are you out of your mind bringing this nut out here? Can't you see that we are on different teams? I've tried your way but God won't have me—no way!"

"Yes, Irene," Tatum pitched in, "There is a way— His Name is Jesus and He will set you free."

"Okay, okay! So you've made your pitch and I ain't buying," I smart mouthed. "Now will you get the hell out of here before I call the police. Hey, somebody bring me another beer and turn up that music. I want to party!"

Inez Simpson and Mrs. Tatum knew they had obeyed God and the rest was between me and Him.

They graciously said goodbye and left, much to my relief.

After an hour and three more beers, I tried getting up from the lounge chair. But something was wrong; my body wouldn't move. I was totally void of strength. Trying not to make a scene, I called softly to Richard, "Come here, please. For some reason, my damn legs won't work. Will you and a couple of the guys help me up?"

They tried standing me on my feet but my legs wouldn't hold me. "I'll be all right," I kept repeating. "I just need a fix to get me going."

So they carried me into Richard's van. One of the guys cooked up some junk and got ready to put the needle into my arm. But as he jabbed it into my flesh, there was no vein. It had collapsed.

"What's wrong with that needle?" I hollered. "Try, try, try! Oh, God, I can't stand the pain. Do something quick, please," I moaned, for by now I was in pure agony.

Finally, they found a vein. As the heroin found its way into the bloodstream, the pain lost its grip and my thoughts broke free, spinning and whirling through my mind. There were flashbacks to my childhood, to my family, back with the Indians; but at every turn, the thought popped up, "Jesus loves you, Irene." I couldn't get away from it.

What seemed like hours later, I began to get a hold of myself. "Irene," I thought, "you can't let yourself go to pieces. There's a good reason for all this." Then it occurred to me that the shots that I had gotten from the doctor to stop my hemorrhaging might have caused this.

I had the guy that had stayed in the van to make sure that I was o.k. get Richard. "Son," I explained, "I'm sure those doctor's shots are what has messed me up. I hate to blow the party, but I think maybe I should get to the doctor."

Richard thought this was a good idea and went into the house to call my doctor for an emergency appointment. The regular physican was out but the nurse referred Richard to another doctor who agreed to help.

By the time we got to the doctor's office, I could hardly move. With my last bit of remaining strength, I rubbed the black polished stone and clalled on the spirits for help. But my mind was much too confused to hear anything. The effect of the heroin was wearing off and I was in pain again.

My condition was very obvious to the doctor. After a brief examination, he said matter-of-factly, "The cause, I believe, for your illness is jaundice. Though your skin is too suntanned to tell, your eyes indicate such a condition in the last stage."

When I explained how tired I was, he replied, "This is not surprising. Your body looks terribly worn. I'm sending you to the hospital right now and I'm prescribing both medical and psychiatric attention. Lady, you are in desperate need of a lot of help."

At the hospital, a panel of doctors began probing, questioning, x-raying and testing every part of my anatomy, it seemed. After they were through, the psychiatrists began working on my mind. "I'm being made some kind of guinea pig," I thought.

But the doctors pretty well all agreed what was wrong with me. The liver, bladder and kidneys were deteriorating; my heart was fixing to give up, my lungs were diseased, and my ears were filled with infection. Their suggested prognosis was nearly hopeless: extensive surgery might prolong life for a short period.

The head psychiatrist overruled this course of action, saying that my mental condition was such that I probably wouldn't survive surgery. So I just lay in bed, either in pain or groggy from medication.

While I was lying in the hospital, Richard and Don, my nephew, had to go to court on the narcotic charges. (Because of my depressed condition, I didn't learn of the outcome until months later.) Don did plead guilty and was sent to prison. Richard was released on probation.

The court date of my trial for possession of drugs arrived but the doctors and psychiatrists would not allow me in court. They told the district attorney that my condition was "that of a vegetable." Therefore, the D.A. dropped my case as well as that against the others since I was the leader.

Even the courts thought I was beyond hope.

CHAPTER 9

SATAN'S LAST FLING

When the doctors had felt they had done all they could do, they sent me home to be with my family. By this time, I was reduced to just 60 pounds of skin and bones. "It is probably in their minds to let me die in peace," I concluded. The psychiatrist prescribed a regular supply of mellaril, to be administered every four hours around the clock. This powerful depressant drug is normally only given to violent mental patients. So it kept me knocked out most of the time.

My family had to feed, bathe and carry me wherever I went. Some of the closer disciples continued to visit me. They would go into the kiva, perform the ceremonial and pray.

My greatest struggle was getting my mind to try to rationalize. Thoughts would last only a moment and then my mind would lapse into nothingness. One moment I'd be listening or sharing in a conversation and the next moment, I'd be delirious. My children didn't know what to do with me.

As every day went by, I would try to hold on to the moments of sanity a little more. I would question the disciples about what was happening: "Have you heard from the spirits?" I would ask. "What do they say about me? Where is the power and help that Satan used to give us?"

When they couldn't answer any of these questions,

I would argue to myself: "Where is all the power, prestige and prosperity now? Here I have dedicated my soul to the evil I've taught, and have faithfully lived the life, and now nothing."

Even when I had the guys cook up some junk and give me a fix, there was no relief from the feelings of death in my mind. The disciples knew something was happening but out of respect for my position as leader and the power I once held, they didn't tell me what they felt or knew—that Satan was killing me.

The psychiatrist increased my medication and suggested I be kept totally quiet. So the children put me in the kiva room. Ordinarily, here it was very quiet and comfortable. Only the more serious minded spiritualists were to be allowed in and the doctors ordered no more drugs other than those prescribed. At first, I thought the change in rooms would be good. "This is great; if the spirits manifest themselves now, I'll be in here to talk and listen to them."

But the first night about midnight, strange things began to happen in the room. Feeling the presence of demonic spirits, I began to call the names of those whom I thought would hear me. "Red Horse! Crafty! Wild Eyes!", I called. "I know you're here in this room. Please answer me!" But there was no manifestation.

"Red Horse, please!" I cried on. "Can't you see that I'm lying here dying in loneliness. You can help me if you want to. I know you can." Still no response.

My daughter came in to give me my medication and I asked her to light some incense to the fire god. "Hope," I said weakly, "Tonight I felt the presence of the spirits. Would you please stay with me for a while and pray?"

Hope nodded but minutes later when she thought I was asleep, she slipped out of the room leaving me alone again. This time I spoke directly to the devil,

"Satan, I deserve an answer to know why and what is happening to me. Haven't I done everything that you have asked me—carrying out your schemes and corruption and teaching your seductions and deceptions? Now look where I am for being your slave? I'm just a mess that nobody, including myself, even wants to look at. My home is now torn apart and destroyed. You have stolen everything I ever had. You liar, all you ever did is lie, lie, lie!"

I moaned on, "Oh, I wish I had never listened to any of your lies! All you want to do is kill me and send me to hell. Will you please spare my children at least? Please, please, spare them all of this terrible hurting agony!"

Hope returned in the middle of this tirade and tried to calm me down. By now my moaning was incomprehensible and it hurt her deeply to see me in agony and not being able to help.

When I gradually quieted down, more out of exhaustion than anything else, Hope thought I would finally get some rest (and hopefully, she too). But the spirits had other plans.

I knew I was dying the death of an infidel; I had heard of others dying in this condition and so fear and torment filled my soul. Sometime in the wee hours, I heard chanting. Then my bed began to shake; there were shrill whistling sounds; then an electric shock and burning around me. The demons were sneering at me and making gurgling sounds. Others were laughing hysterically. I experienced stinging and pains shooting through my body like electric shocks. When I tried to scream out for help, no sounds would come out.

Presently, furniture started falling over and my bed was shaking like it was in an earthquake. Hope heard the commotion and came in. She flicked on the light and just stared in unbelief at the mess the demons had created. "Hope," I said, "you've gotta get me out of this room! Please don't leave me in here any longer!"

Hope went and got Richard and together they prepared for me an old bedroom overlooking the backyard which I had once used for meditation. The room was dark and dreary and in my death-like condition, I matched its appearance to a tee.

The children discouraged anyone but closest members of the clan from seeing me. All partying in the house was kept to a minimum and done quietly to keep from disturbing me. One day they did allow one of the young female clan members to bring her sister in to visit me. As I tried to speak to greet her, a horrible sound came out of my throat. The sister fainted on the spot and had to be carried out.

Oh, how I hated what I had become! It seemed that I was in hell already. But where there is still breath, there is hope. And better things were soon to happen. . .

CHAPTER 10

THE GENTLE VOICE OF GOD

The voice was clear and distinct: "Irene, you are dying. This is it."

It was mid-afternoon and everything was unusually quiet. The children and some of the clan members were just outside in the sitting room. Hope had come in to check on me, but believing that I was resting, she didn't give me my medication and went out leaving me alone.

I knew I was alone but here was this gentle voice again, calling my name. I strained to listen and repeatedly the Spirit of God related the same message, "Irene, you are dying."

The words pierced my soul as a two-edged sword. My heart cried out to my mind, "I don't want to die like this." And suddenly, I was praying and pleading outloud, "God, please don't let me die like this; I am lost! Oh, God, I'll go to hell. Please help me! God, please don't let me go to hell! I beg you, God. Forgive me, Lord Jesus!"

I don't know how I got off that bed and out to the sitting room but it had to be by the help of the angels of God. For at the time, I was so weak that I couldn't even hold a glass of water. So the children just stared in disbelief as I pushed open the door and crawled out of the bedroom on my hands and knees to where they were sitting.

"Mama," said Hope after a moment. "What do you want anyway?"

I fought their efforts to help. There was just one thought that grew stronger and clearer in my mind—to get back to God. As Hope and a friend tried against my resistance to lift me off the floor, I told them, "I've got to get back to God. I cannot die like this. Oh, God, please forgive me! Please don't send me to hell! God, I'm begging you to help me!"

The girls were holding up my shoulders while I was sitting on my knees, praying. But I was oblivious to everything around me because in that moment the Spirit of God came on and in me with a shower of heavenly love. The anguish lifted, the hurting went and I was divinely strengthened and put in my right mind.

For maybe a minute or two, I just sat there as waves of peace and refreshment flowed over me. And then there was the gentle voice again. It said, "Go see Theresa McAllister." Theresa was an evangelist that I had known slightly, years before when I first had tried to be a Christian.

Opening my eyes, I said to Hope, "I'd like to go see Theresa McAllister. Will you call and try to reach her?"

Hope called and found out that Theresa was holding a tent revival in a little community less that twenty miles from our house. She agreed to come out to the tent early and meet us there. So together Hope and Richard and the others bundled me up and got me into the car and off we went.

Theresa was there waiting for us when we arrived. I told her how God had reached down and touched my life and that now I wanted to get to the altar to confess Christ Jesus before men.

Richard carried me to the altar and knelt with

me as I continued to pour out my heart before God. My tear ducts were still bottled up, but inside me there was a flood of light bursting into my dark, dry and bitter soul. A deeper release from my burdens and sins came as I started to thank Jesus.

Theresa came around the front of the altar and we praised God together. Then she lifted up my weak arms and hands toward heaven and said, "Sweet Jesus, now baptize my dear sister with the Holy Ghost."

Immediately, I started speaking in a heavenly language. Oh, what a release! Oh, what a strengthening in my heart! Though I didn't know the scripture at the time, I was experiencing exactly what the apostle Paul wrote the Romans in the eighth chapter, "Likewise the Spirit also helped our infirmities: for we know not what we should pray for as we ought: but the Spirit itself maketh intercession for us with groanings that cannot be uttered." The Holy Spirit was taking my hurts, confusion and sin and lifting it from me to God's great throne of mercy. How good it felt!

I would have liked to stay there for hours but by now people were coming in to start the service. When Richard helped me up, a new creature walked out of that tent. I knew that I was saved and that my soul was bound for heaven.

Everyone that saw me that night heard my bubbling confession of joy, "Christ Jesus has forgiven me. Satan has lost this soul. I am saved and going to heaven." Likely, some of the people thought I had lost my mind and had gone crazy but in reality, "Crazy Irene" died that night and a new Irene, pure and righteous, was born.

As we rode through the countryside back to Tampa that evening, I suddenly realized that God's goodness was everywhere: the beautiful trees and flowers, animals and birds. "Hallelujah, Hallelujah!" I cried to the mighty God.

Back in the house, however, I realized that the victory had been won but the battle wasn't over yet. For some forty years the devil had claimed me as his own and now he was not about to give up. My yielding to Christ simply meant that the battle over my soul was now out in the open.

Hardly had Hope said goodnight and turned off the light in my bedroom when every tormentor in hell it seemed came to prey upon me. God had come into my life but that didn't stop the demons from harassing me from without. I knew nothing then about spiritual warfare, but I learned that first night that calling upon the name of Jesus brought both protection and relief from the attacks of the enemy.

Now, there are many Christians that believe once you come to Christ, you cannot be possessed by a demon. I would not argue over terms or theology, but I know there were demons, both outside my mind and inside my mind, outside my body and inside my body— and all seemed determined to either keep me as their possession or else kill me altogether.

As I struggled to oppose and live, I began to discover how really dead I was in mind and body. I had lost practically all of my natural emotions, parts of both my mind and body were numb, and I could not cry and had not done so in over six years.

Even closing my eyes to try to sleep was a desperate struggle. I had to physically push them shut with my hands to get them to close. My soul had become so yielded to the devil and his demonic spirits that they seemed to have more control over my body than me. Now that I was in Christ, I had to struggle and fight to regain control of my mind and body. But in this battle, thank God, I wasn't alone. The Spirit of God was there, encouraging me and strengthening me against the demons so that "me could get back in me."

Several times that first week it seemed that dawn

would come before the demons would let up their attack and allow me to sleep. But each night I could tell that I was getting stronger and more stable. And soon there were others around to help.

At my request, Richard called one of my old friends, Faith Ponton, and told her the good news that "I had come back to Jesus." Faith got so excited that she couldn't resist coming to see me and bringing with her another mutual friend named Carmen.

As happy as they were to see me and hear about my conversion, my appearance was a shock to them, for no one outside the immediate family knew of my deteriorating health. But they came near and hugged my neck. Faith said, "Irene, we love you and we know God is going to keep and protect you."

After some more sharing and encouragement, Carmen and Faith prayed for God to touch my mind. They anointed my body with oil according to God's promise in James chapter five and asked God to deliver me. And their kindness wasn't just in words.

Faith offered to come and stay in the house so she could personally wait on me. Because she insisted that Jesus wanted her to do this, I couldn't refuse. She stayed with me day and night. When I would cry out because of the torment of the demons, she would come in the bedroom, pray and read the Bible until I calmed down and the demons left.

The spirits were persistent and didn't give up easily, even with Faith around. In me, through me and outside of me, they would throw things around, pull at me, shake my bed, open and close doors—anything to keep me from resting. Often when they were controlling me, I would yell at Faith and resist her efforts on my behalf. Thank God, Faith knew it wasn't me doing this but the devils inside me. So she would simply bind the devils in the Name of Jesus and try to draw me back to my right mind by repeating again and again, "Irene, I love you so much and Jesus loves you, too." God's love was overcoming the demons within.

Faith started bringing Bibles into my room and leaving them open. Soon the whole house looked like wall to wall Bibles! There were thick ones and thin ones, new ones and old ones. Faith even placed them on top of my body and underneath the sheets. At night when she'd want to rest, she would plug in the cassette recorder with Bible tapes playing near my bed so that I could hear the Word.

Without fully realizing it, Faith was doing what the Bible commands and was utilizing the most powerful weapon a Christian has against the deceit and power of the devil. For the Apostle Paul declares in II Corinthians 10:4, 5: "For the weapons of our warfare are not carnal, but mighty through God to the pulling down of strong holds; casting down imaginations, and every high thing that exalteth itself against the knowledge of God, and bringing every thought to the obedience of Christ."

Gradually, God's Word was tearing down those satanic strongholds in my mind—replacing them with the word of faith—"faith comes by hearing and hearing by the Word of God." The fruit of Faith's obedience to the Spirit of God was that I began to sleep much easier. My experience began to line up with Solomon's, who declared in Proverbs 3:24, that when we fill our minds with the words of life, "When thou liest down, thou shalt not be afraid: yea, thou shalt lie down, and thy sleep shall be sweet."

Meanwhile, there were many prayer groups in the area that were lifting me up before the throne of God. From Faith, I learned that several prayer warriors were faithfully praying for my salvation even before I came back to God. Undoubtedly, this had much to do with God's mercy on me.

One of these precious people, Vivian Faircloth, a

sister in Christ that I knew, had fasted for many days for God to keep me and bring me back. Satan had tried to discourage her and get her to quit praying for me but she persisted. The day that I fell before God in repentance is the day that Vivian came off her fast. God spoke to her that her prayer was going to be answered and I would be saved.

Many Christians, some that I never met, sent messages of kindness and encouragement. Then as I grew stronger, Faith would let them in to see me. Some of my former disciples also came by but they quickly discovered that I had "changed teams" and left.

Those first three months Faith was my guardian angel and without her, I felt lost and threatened. Occasionally, when she would have to go out to do shopping or errands, the demons would have a hayday—harassing me with all kinds of strange noises and rocking, bouncing and pulling on my bed. When she would return, I'd plead with her never to leave me alone again.

One day Faith determined that I was ready for a new challenge. "Irene," she said, "today you're going to take a shower by yourself." I started to protest. "But—" Faith cut me off. "Now, Irene, with Christ, you can do it. You have nothing to be afraid of."

So I agreed to try. As soon as the shower door was closed behind me, the forces of evil began to appear, manifesting themselves as ugly little animals, trying to sting me. "Help, please help!" I screamed. "They're attacking me and I can't get away."

By the time Faith got the door open, I was hysterical, down on my knees, pleading the blood of Jesus. Faith joined me in praying in tongues and as quickly as the demons had come, they disappeared. Another of so many battles had been won. But I'm sure Faith was wondering just like I was, "When would I totally get delivered and set free?"

CHAPTER 11

DELIVERANCE

Ever since Faith had come to stay with me, she had been praying and fasting off and on for my deliverance. One major obstacle was the fact that my mind and body were saturated with drugs. It wasn't that I wanted to take the medication. I wanted to trust Jesus and be free. But both of us weren't quite sure what would happen if I stopped taking the pills.

Some of the evil spirits that were inside of me had been there since the age of three. And the fact that I had come to Christ once and turned away, my fate was seven times worse than it would have been otherwise. I desperately wanted to be free from both the drugs and the demons, but I trusted Faith's discernment from God to know when I was strong enough to receive and keep my deliverance.

It may have been that God used the incident in the shower to confirm to Faith that it was now time for the big showdown with Satan. Anyway, the very next day, Faith told me after we had finished our Bible reading, "Today we are starting your deliverance. So there is going to be no more medication. We are going to trust Jesus for total victory for you. Now it's not going to be easy but remember, 'greater is He, Christ in you, than he that is in the world.' We are going to defeat Satan totally in your life."

As we prayed, Faith first covered us with the blood

of Jesus. Then she took authority over all the forces of evil that would oppose the Spirit of God. Under the anointing of the Holy Spirit, she began to name the spirits and demand that they leave my body. Each time she did this and a demon would leave, I would feel stronger and more in control of my life.

Because many of the demons were stubborn and refused to leave without a struggle, several sessions were required. When I would get physically drained and weak, Faith would let me rest for the day. And then it would start again the next day. Each day I was getting stronger spiritually and freer mentally.

The chief liar, as you might have guessed, was Red Horse . . . and he fought to keep his claims on me. He would declare, "Irene, you must come back to us. You can't believe Faith or any of those Christians. If you come back now, everything will be all right. Otherwise, we'll have to torture you."

One of his emissaries would make the sounds of swinging chains trying to scare me (we had been into the martial arts). Others continued their harassing of slamming doors, throwing objects and making shrill noises. In the middle of this, the devil would say, "If you don't come back, you are not going to live. You swore your soul to me so it's mine forever." When I would share these things with Faith, she would take authority over the devil and reassure me of God's mercy.

As much as I needed God's strength, Faith needed it even more, so she could minister to me. The only way she could do this was to get alone with God. And sometimes I wondered how she could keep on and if I ever would be completely delivered.

Faith called other prayer warriors and asked them to join her in prayer as she ministered to me. I know this really helped because one day Red Horse had me seriously doubting my salvation and deliverance and the next day, I knew clearly that he was a liar and that he had to leave my life in the mighty name of Jesus. Just that quickly and easily, the one that influenced and controlled my life for as long as I could remember was gone from my life. And I didn't miss him at all. I was free! Death had been swallowed up in victory—the victorious life I was experiencing in Jesus Christ.

Through the power of God and the persevering prayers of the saints to whom I will ever be grateful, I was free. In those first weeks and months, that freedom was often severely tested and tried. When it got out that I was physically well, the old satanic disciples began to come by, more and more. They would tempt me with drugs and all sorts of evil and make like I was really flipped out when I would share my experience in Christ.

But, thank God, I began to discover that I was no longer bound by other people. I had tasted of reality for myself and had discovered the real Way of Life and nobody was about to turn me aside from the Way.

I began to see the lies beyond the glittering facade of Satan's temptations and by the Spirit of God, his deceit and lies were easy to see. With this new understanding, I could now look back on past experiences and see how I was twisted into believing a lie and maybe help someone else from falling into the same trap.

CHAPTER 12

A PERVERSE SPIRIT

During those years that I was backslidden from God, I had been involved in pornographic and obscene movie-making. In this, I participated with people of all ages, color, and economic and cultural status. The more perverted the material, the greater the demand and the pay.

My conscience in this area was twisted and seared from the time I was a young child. I was certainly not clear of fault for entering this web of gross sin but then circumstances played a large part.

First, at home, I saw essentially no expression of love exhibited between my mother and father so I never saw what a normal, healthy love relationship between a man and a woman was like.

Further, without any parental guidance in this area, at the age of seven or eight, I was introduced to lesbian behavior by an older girl named Sharon. I participated in homosexuality with Sharon out of curiosity and continued in it to maintain her friendship. My hatred toward the police because of their treatment to my dad and failure at three marriages instilled in me nothing but contempt for men and kept me from experiencing anything fulfilling in the realm of human love. There was no thought or inkling of pleasure in giving myself to a man or a woman; the only pleasure involved was the thought of either seducing a person, making more money or experiencing the adventure of performing some more grotesque sexual perversion. This is how twisted my mind had become.

When I finally returned to Jesus, the devils tried to condemn me and threaten me with exposure if I didn't return to Satan's fold. But, thank God, I realized this, too, was under the blood of Jesus, who had cleansed me of *all* sin. Not only that, but now that I was free I could look back into my past and see the horrible pit that I was in (and thank God for His delivering me).

From Sharon I learned firsthand about the cunningness of a person with a homosexual (perverse spirit) drive. There is a seducing spirit about them that breeds immorality and corruption and endeavors to enslave everyone they touch. The way that homosexuals play upon their prey is like an animal stalking their catch.

Once a person is enslaved in its web, the same seducing spirit comes on him or her and entices that person to ensnare others. So unless one comes to Jesus, it is almost impossible to ever get free of this sin. Many times before I came to Christ I tried to go straight but the perverse spirit always drew me back into the grips of this degradation. I came to think that I was destined to be homosexual. This is one of the biggest lies that Satan has perpetuated today—that one is born or destined to be a homosexual. Like anyone else, I grew up with many questions about my sexual identity. Because of the influence of external circumstances and the suggestions of demonic spirits, I chose to believe a lie and identify myself with this sin.

Now, thank God, our Lord doesn't condemn us when in our ignorance we fall into sin. But neither does He condone our continuing in sinful behavior after we are shown the way of Truth.

God doesn't make mistakes and the Bible tells us

that we have been called and predestined from the foundation of the world. The Lord reminded Jeremiah that He had called him while he was still in his mother's womb. So God knows and plans our purpose and sexual identity. And He will reveal it to us if we but submit to His will.

God's judgment of homosexual activity as sin is very clear in the Bible. As far back as the days of Abraham, God condemned homosexual activity, destroying the cities of Sodom and Gomorrah for this sin. Old Testament law declared, "Thou shalt not lie with mankind, as with womankind: it is abomination" (Lev. 18:22). Penalty for disobedience was death by stoning.

In the New Testament, the apostle Paul wrote to the Romans what could happen to the man who denied the reality of God: "For this cause God gave them up unto vile affections: for even their women did change the natural use into that which is against nature: And likewise also the men, leaving the natural use of the woman, burned in their lust one toward another; men with men working that which is unseemly, and receiving in themselves that recompence of their error which was meet. And even as they did not like to retain God in their knowledge, God gave them over to a reprobate mind" (Rom. 1:26-28).

This surely happened in my life as when I turned from God, my mind became totally given over to thoughts of greed and lust. Thank God for those saints who didn't give up totally on me but in their witness planted new seeds of truth that brought me back from the pit.

There are those who say that once a person has become a homosexual and his mind is reprobate that there is no more hope for their salvation. This is neither true in my experience nor in Paul's writing to the Corinthians where he says, "Know ye not that the unrighteous shall not inherit the kingdom of God? Be not deceived: neither fornicators, nor idolators, nor adulterers, nor effeminate, nor abusers of themselves with mankind [homosexuals]... shall inherit the kingdom of God. And such were some of you, but ye are washed, but ye are sanctified, but ye are justified in the name of the Lord Jesus" (I Cor. 6:9-11).

Learned sinful behavior can be forgiven, cleansed and unlearned as God by His Grace brings us out of darkness into His glorious light. When I came to Christ with my whole heart, He not only forgave me but set me free of the perverse spirit that drove me to homosexual sin. Then as I opened my heart to the counsel of the Holy Spirit, our Divine Teacher, He began to show me how to rightly love (not lust after) others and develop wholesome relationships in Him.

Not only did God do this for me but He has allowed me to pray with several other "homosexuals" to experience this same deliverance. If you happen to be caught in this same sin, I believe that God will do the same for you that He did for me. Simply repent of this evil, and call on God's forgiveness and mercy. He will both save and deliver!

CHAPTER 13

THE SIN OF WITCHCRAFT

America, perhaps more than any nation in the world, was founded on principles of faith and truth based on the true and living God. In our pledge of allegiance, we declare ourselves to be "one nation under God." On our money, we proclaim, "In God we trust."

Into this society, a television show "innocently" proclaimed that a kind "genie" witch could perform good miraculous feats for her friends. And then pretty soon an innocent looking board game offers wisdom from the realm of the spirits. Before long, the biggest box office movie hits are bombarding our children with satanic babies, powers and destruction. A popular soap opera daily visits into clairvoyance, spiritism, and psychic powers. Saturday morning cartoons feature superhuman heroes with powers from the spirit world. Suddenly, the occult has become commonplace. How has this happened in America?

One does not have to be a genius or a prophet to recognize that in the early sixties, Americans largely deferred its leadership to youth in the area of music, arts, entertainment, and even government. We became a youth culture and a largely rebellious youth culture at that. What does the Bible say about rebellion? I Samuel 15:23 declares, "Rebellion is as the sin of witchcraft." It is no coincidence that once we accepted rebellion, our society became deluged with witchcraft. Satan is the crafty author of both.

Make no mistake to think that witchcraft and its current expressions in our society are the result of some innocent fad. Revelation 12:12 declares that in these last days Satan, "knowing that he hath but a short time, worketh a great wrath." And so it is today.

Nearly all the spreading of occult practice in America is being done by people that are firmly in the hands of the devil who, in exchange for power and wealth, have fully yielded their souls to his work.

There is a definite power structure in satanic order. To be able to work up the ladder in Satan's domain, a person must consecrate his entire being to evil. To perform the supernatural power of darkness, one must devote time to study and meditation. Everything that Satan offers is a counterfeit of the real thing. If one will devote himself to the devil, he promises to give that person power, wealth and authority—not the real thing but power based on fear instead of love; wealth in money but not in the soul; and authority based on deceit rather than truth.

However, once a person is deceived and starts toward the bait that Satan dangles before him (like I did), it becomes a long road of darkness. Satan is always there offering a little more power, a little more greed—as the Bible says, "The eyes of the wicked are never satisfied" (Prov. 27:20).

The higher (or actually lower) a person climbs in one's search for power and control in Satan's domain, the more possessed and controlled by the devil that person becomes. As the wicked are not satisfied, neither are Satan's angels: "Hell and destruction are not full" (Prov. 27:20). The demons' mission and goal are to steal and destroy and they will never be satisfied until they have stolen the soul and destroyed the body and mind of the person in their hands.

Yet, this is not to say that satanists and witches are not without order or organization. Actually, most satanic cults are highly organized with a definite, though secretive, order of leadership. The demons use this structure of order to entice members in thirst for more power—which leads the captive deeper into Satan's control.

In many ways, witches' covens and satanic cults are not much different from most mystical orders and brotherhoods, secretive sisterhoods, fraternities and sororities, all of whom are based on secret covenants. With satanists, however, there is no morality, self-discipline or benevolent goals. There is no such thing as a good or white witch (this is another demonic deception).

A witch must submit not only his own soul, body and spirit to the devil but also his family (if married) to also be used as tools and vessels of Satan at his discretion. Based on the creeds and vows made during the secret initiation ceremonies in most satanic orders, the devil has every legal right to use (or dispose of) the person or any member of his family for his purposes. It is much like playing Russian roulette with your soul.

Curiosity and adventure draw the interest of many people into these satanic cults but it is usually thirst for power that holds them in this fatalistic snare. In the satanic order of leadership, a person may move up to Potentate, High Potentate, Supreme Pontiff, and finally High Priest or Priestess. In our coven, I was the High Priestess when Christ Jesus saved me.

When the demons realized that I was not going to be drawn back into the clan, no doubt I was ordered to be destroyed. Not only did the demons try to kill me themselves with their harassment, but I'm sure that they encouraged other members of the clan to kill me. The person that would kill or dispose of me would become the likely candidate to take my place as leader.

Only the supernatural power of God protected me from certain death those first few months that I was saved. Faith prayed daily that God would cover me with His divine protection. Often, when clan members came to visit me, I literally feared for my life. But, I discovered that "greater is He [Christ] in me than he that is in the world." And I was never harmed.

For a person involved in satanic worship or demonic activity, God's protection will not, however, cover er him unless he first renounces and repents of all his satanic activities. If anyone reading this book is now involved and now wants to be free of this curse, the following prayer, prayed from the heart, will bring deliverance and God's protection:

> "In the Name of Jesus, I renounce my participation in all satanic orders, cults and mystical brotherhoods. I also renounce all vows that bind me and my family to any satanic order, sect or clan. I repent of this sin and ask the blood of Jesus to cleanse and nullify and make void the vows I made and now loose me from them.

> "Lord, I now praise and thank You that You have come to deliver me and give me freedom from the power of Satan. I now command Satan in Jesus' Name to loose his influence upon me and all the members of my family. Thank You, Jesus. Amen."

There is no power that Satan has over the truly submitted child of God in right relationship with Jesus! Oh, how that message of God's power needs to be preached from our pulpits today. One of Jesus' self-confessed anointings of the Spirit of God which He gave in Luke 4:18 was "to preach deliverance to the captives." If more of God's servants were obedient to the Spirit of God in this area today, our mental hospitals wouldn't be so crowded and the Body of Christ would be healthier and happier.

Additionally, if America is ever to again be free of satanic practice and the curse of occultism, Christian ministers and lay people alike must "stand up and speak the Truth"—what the Bible says about the occult. The Bible is literally full of admonition against participation in the occult, yet never once did I hear such from a Christian before my conversion and deliverance.

From the time of Moses, God declared that all forms of fortunetelling, spiritism, magic practices and involvement in the cults and their teachings are absolutely forbidden: " . . . thou shalt not learn to do after the abomination of those nations. There shall not be found with thee any one . . . that useth divination (fortune telling), or an observer of times (soothsayer), or an enchanter (magician), or a witch, or a charmer (hypnotist), or a consulter with familiar spirits, or a wizard (clairvoyant or psychic), or a necromancer (medium who consults the dead). For all that do these things are an ABOMINATION unto the Lord!" (Deut. 18:9-12).

The New Testament reinforces and emphasizes this language—allowing no mercy for those who continue in the occult, warning that "they which do such things shall not inherit the kingdom of God" (Gal. 5:19-21) and " . . . shall have their part in the lake which burneth with fire and brimstone" (Rev. 21:8).

If we don't want our children and youth deceived and ensnared by the subtlety of Satan, we must admonish and warn them often of these truths. God's Word has all the power and protection we need! And God's Spirit is wholly capable of leading us into all truth—as I was to experience daily in a wonderful way.

CHAPTER 14

THE LEAVEN HUNT

I was set free! I knew it. No longer was I Satan's tool. Jesus Christ had freed me from my horrible past and had set me on the solid rock, the Truth. Yet for some reason, sleep would not come—for hours, sometimes even days.

I'd been saved and delivered now for several months and knew that through Christ I had power over the devil and his angels. Since my nerves were acting up terribly, the slightest noise would upset me. Neither Faith nor I could understand what was happening to me. But we did think God's Spirit might be trying to tell us something.

One day Faith asked, "Why don't we try fasting for seven days or as long as you can? I believe if you do this, God will show us what is the problem."

"O.K.", I said, "I've got nothing to lose. I'll try as long as I can."

On the third day of our fast, a friend of Faith's called and said the night before she had had a dream. Since she knew something of my past, she thought the dream might have some significance to me. In it, she saw the powers of Satan chaining a person to a stake. All around were Indian artifacts and in the midst were Indians worshipping idols.

When Faith related this to me, I instantly knew this was God speaking because her friend knew nothing of the vast collection of Indian artifacts and lore that I accumulated. Along with these, the altar and ceremonial offerings to the gods remained in the kiva room.

We both knew there had been demonic activity among the artifacts in my bedroom and in the kiva. There had been objects that had moved and been knocked around. Weird noises could be heard at night; it had to be the spirits at work. So we agreed to dispose of the entire collection, immediately.

Faith borrowed a wheelbarrow and we loaded it with tomahawks, axes, grinding stones, pottery, granite hatchets, arrowheads, fetishes of stone and jewelry, beadwork and the clothing which I had used in the ritual ceremonies, tribal dances and worship. Now when I was leader of our satanic clan, I thought I had thrown some fine parties, but this was clearly the best ever.

Here were Faith and I trooping around the house, singing songs of praise to Jesus to the top of our lungs and picking up all these precious, expensive trinkets and smashing them into that old wheelbarrow. Anyone outside would have thought we were crazy for sure but we were having a ball. Even the children, Richard and Hope, joined in the fun and helped us gather the articles and sing praises to Jesus.

Determined that no one else would ever fall into the snare of idolatry from these articles, we made sure each item was either smashed to bits and thrown in the river or anything flammable was stacked in a pile to be burned.

What a fire Richard built! We had an old pit out back and Richard prepared a roaring fire for us. As each rug or piece of clothing or wooden artifact was thrown into the fire, we lifted up another song or chorus of praise to the Lord Jesus. We knew the Lord was gaining a mighty victory and we were going to give Him all the glory.

Faith prayed and asked the Lord that not a single thread that represented the old Irene would remain. And as she prayed, a very gentle breeze blew over causing the fire to blaze. What a wonderful confirmation that God's hand had destroyed the works of darkness. And from that day, my sleep improved and my nerves began to heal.

The climax to our party came a couple of days later when a friend showed us from the Bible in Acts 19:19 that what we were doing was scriptural, that it was exactly what the new believers (ex-sorcorers) in Ephesus had done: "Many of them also which used curious arts brought their books together, and burned them before all men: and they counted the price of them and found it fifty thousand pieces of silver."

So as the Lord gave me strength and guidance, I began sorting through the books in our library. There were books on bloodless teachings, satanic worship, spiritualism, and the psychic works of Tom Pain, Edgar Cayce, Charles Filmore and others. Others included books on how to save yourself, eastern cult literature, meditation, mind expansion, astral projection and mind control. Each one of these books offered a way to success through the building up and perfecting of self. But in the end, each way only leads to destruction because in reality man's worst enemy and biggest stumbling block to life and success is his own self nature.

Thus, the Bible declares, "There is a (broad) way that seems right to a man but the end thereof is death." The way to success and life is the way of the cross— death to self but new and eternal life in Christ.

After we had sorted out all the cult and self-oriented books (encompassing most of the library), another bonfire was built. Then came the tearing, ripping, burning and more praising the Lord. As the books went up in a great and odorous cloud of smoke, there was another great release in my spirit.

Even then, we discovered we weren't through "clearing the air" in the house. For our satanic rituals and séances, we always used fire and incense. So Faith and I proceeded to gather up all the incense burners and the images of gods that burned incense from every room in the house. We carried them out and threw them on the book bonfire and later buried the remains once the fire was out.

Believing that we had completely cleaned everything out, I expected a new peace and freedom to fill the house. But the next night, I awoke around midnight under such oppression that I thought I would die. Faith came in and prayed and in a short while I felt better again.

The very next day our friend, Carmen, called and shared a vision that the Lord had given her. She said, "I saw little ugly men going back and forth from Hope's room to yours, working evil against you and trying to keep you from being healed. When I saw this, I asked the Lord what was causing it. His messenger then showed me a vase made of brass and filled with articles of evil and corruption. There must be some kind of vase in the the house that you have overlooked."

Carmen was right! There in Hope's room was the vase just like the Lord had shown her. In it were feathers, a fetish, and a small ceremonial pouch. When we opened it, out came a pile of amphetimine pills (uppers). Faith exclaimed, "I would have never thought to look here, would you?"

I shook my head and replied, "But then God never makes a mistake, does He?" I was really beginning to believe this and it made me feel so good inside to think that God cared so much for my welfare.

The one person that was none too happy about this experience was Hope. It turned out that the pills were hers and when she found out we had destroyed them, she about raised the roof with her fury. She, at that time, had not come back to the Lord and her anger was not really her's but the devil's, who did not like being found out. In time, Hope would come to appreciate my obedience to God and surrender to God herself.

Our final leaven hunt brought us to a workshop on the grounds where we found more drugs, bong pipes and marijuana. These were all destroyed or flushed down the toilet. For so long, God had nothing in my life, now I was determined to give Him everything.

With the complete cleansing of these outer forms of evil, the Lord began to do a deeper and more important work within my life. He impressed on my heart to start forgiving everyone that the Holy Spirit would bring to my remembrance. As I did this, I found that it was necessary to also forgive myself. After all the evil things that I had been a part of, this was perhaps the most difficult task that God put before me. God is faithful and long-suffering and as the weeks passed, layer upon layer of unforgiveness and bitterness were unravelled and cleansed away.

Finally, the root of bitterness came to the surface. I had to forgive all of the people that had hurt my daddy, so God could forgive me. There was nothing inside of me that wanted to do this. It would have to be God.

As I struggled with this, the Holy Spirit seemed to say, "I will help you if you really want Me to." I realized God was patiently waiting on my obedience. "God, You've been so good to me," I cried. "Yes, I do want Your forgiveness for holding this hurt in my heart all these years. I forgive the policemen and I forgive Daddy for leaving us. And now, God, please forgive me."

Never before or since have I heard the audible voice of God. But in that moment, it was as if God was standing right beside me, saying, "You are forgiven; now forgive yourself."

Oh, what joy came surging through me! What peace came over me. I had been smoking three or more packs of cigarettes a day and in that moment, the Holy Spirit set me free from that bondage also.

Victory surged through my very soul. I was free! My health renewed like springtime and my strength soared like an eagle. Death was swallowed up in victory!

CHAPTER 15

EXPOSING SATAN'S GAMES

With the root of bitterness and unforgiveness gone, Satan no longer had any place in me, inside or out. I was free—free to see the truth and free to be a servant of the Lord. Now I could say with Christ, "Satan cometh and he has no place in me."

Now that I was free, I could begin to minister to others that were still caught in the same web of deception that had bound me for forty long years. One of the first things that God called me to do as I began to minister for Him was to expose Satan's games—not only to help deliver the ensnared but to protect the uninformed from falling into the same snare.

"Witch On Trial For Murder" read the recent newspaper headline in the Plainview Texas Daily. What started out as some curious fun for five teenagers wanting to visit a witches' house on Halloween night ended with fifteen-year-old Roxanne Cases brutally executed by a satanic high priest.

This is not an isolated case out of the past. It is a current happening reoccurring over and over today in America. What most Americans, and unfortunately many in our churches, pass off as a harmless, spooky time for tricks and treats is in reality one of the most subtle and deadly schemes of the devils.

Despite the Bible's clear admonition to "give no place to the devil," Halloween night was originally celebrated within churches as a night to pacify the demon spirits. How sad this is—after our Lord Jesus Christ suffered and died to totally defeat Satan for us, His church goes and surrenders to a defeated foe!

No wonder Satan and his angels celebrate on Halloween! On this day the satanic powers and passions of evil and wickedness and corruption run rampant among satanists. Usually there is a mass celebration where blood sacrifices are offered. It may be an animal or even the life of a baby or child.

In our own clan, we took the satanic celebration on Halloween very seriously—respecting the desires of the spirits and obeying their instructions for the celebration of this day implicitly. One Halloween when a couple of the members of our clan got careless, it almost cost them their lives.

On this particular Halloween, I had put two of our girls, Joyce and Betty, in charge of the preparations and had given them very simple instructions of what to do. But they decided they would do it their own way and have a little fun.

Instead of fixing the kettle of oil in private, they set it up right in the front yard. Out there showing off, they started preparing the animal sacrifice (killing and skinning a cat). And in the window, they lit the black candles without permission.

When I returned and saw what was happening, I was appalled and knew the spirits would be angry. After chastising the girls and getting everything back in order, I went into the kiva to try to appease the spirits. The demons of the winds and earth appeared and commanded the offering of life. I begged for mercy that the lives of the girls be spared. Well, later that night a hurricane rose up in the Tampa area and gale winds wrecked havoc right in the area where the girls lived. While their lives were spared, their home was made a shambles. It made an indelible impression on them.

Perhaps even more deadly than the violent practices of the Satanist groups like ours on Halloween is the subtle deception practiced by the world on this "holiday" which says that it is fun and right to dress up in costumes and play mean to get what you want. Because of this idea, many young people were drawn into our clan, thinking at first that it was nothing more than a glorified Halloween party. The younger a person is when Satan gets a hold of him, the more pliable and usable for demonic practices he will be. So Satan makes his greatest pitches for the young. In our clan, before many youth knew what was happening, they were initiated and their soul was sold to the devil.

The Bible doesn't talk about "Satan coming as an angel of light" without good reason. Most all of Satan's works are forms of counterfeiting the reality of God. All of the false religions and cults are based on this. These false religions will take a truth of God and twist it in Satan's hands and suddenly there arises Mormonism, Unity, Moonies, the Children of God, Hare Krishna, Mohammedanism, Christian Science, Jehovah's Witnesses, Buddhism, and the like.

Man is born with a spiritual hunger inside to know and fellowship with his Creator, God. If this hunger is not satisfied through a personal relationship with Jesus Christ, Satan will come and deceive with a counterfeit. How many of the occult practices are Satan's subtle tricks to make us think we are reaching the divine! Astrology, hypnotism, Ouija boards, tarot cards, crystal ball gazing, palm reading, psychic healing, charming, soul travel, mind expansion, and ESP are all out of Satan's bag of tricks.

Having practiced and taught each of these subtle

games and schemes, I know the bewitching power behind them. Anyone who has in any way been involved in any of these things should immediately renounce them, repent and ask Jesus to forgive and cleanse them from any effect they might still have.

Another of the more subtle ways Satan comes as an angel of light is to perform miracles, counterfeiting the things of God. Demonic spirits can and do appear to perform good as long as it is needed to accomplish the deceptions to which they are sent. This is why the Holy Spirit gives the gift of discernment to members in the Body of Christ to discern the spirits. Many times Satan will infiltrate a weak Christian or non-believer to cause havoc in a Christian body.

The Bible says that we should not be ignorant of his (Satan's) devices. It is obvious that Satan as the great counterfeiter is not ignorant of God's ways! As the highest priestess of our coven, I led many séances. The structure of the séance is very similar to that of a Christian prayer meeting. We even called the inner sanctum of worship for the most select and dedicated disciples the Unholy of Unholies. In the séance (sometimes practiced in the nude and other times not), we would usually form a circle under a bright light. Everyone would sit quietly at first until all was still and sensitive to the spirits and powers of evil. Some members would pray quietly and then the medium would pray.

Either the medium or another person who was very sensitive to the spirits would go into a trance. His face would become distorted and change features as the evil spirit would manifest itself and take control.

In those sittings, it would not be unusual for a person to be there who was seeking contact with a dead loved one. If so, the features of the medium would change, even the color of the eyes would appear like the loved one which was being called forth. Although there would be no real manifestation of the dead either in spirit or in body, the subtlety of Satan could make it seem very convincing to the unlearned.

Clairvoyance had been a regular part of our séance practices. A clairvoyant is a medium who sees supernaturally, and I was very proud of my "gift" in this area, even during the period when I was using drugs heavily. But I wasn't the only such medium in our group. Regularly, we sought the spirits about coming events and how and when to do certain things. We trusted this demonic information implicitly.

According to satanic practice, satanic knowledge and wisdom come from vibrations through handling an object or article that belonged to the person in question. These vibrations are given by familiar spirits who knew in intimate detail all about the person. The familiar spirits will even mimic the person's voice through the medium.

Other manifestations in the séances would counterfeit the real gifts of the Holy Spirit. Through psychic prayer there were "miracles" of objects moving through space, "apparent healings," and even a form of speaking in an unknown language and interpretation.

Our particular coven was openly satanistic. But there was essentially no difference from our séances and those of groups of spiritualists who claim to be in contact with the divine. In all groups where a medium is involved, one can be certain that evil spirits are at the foundation. The Bible says that there is but one intermediary between God and man—and that is Christ Jesus our Lord! (1 Tim. 2:5).

If we know this and keep our life centered in Christ, we will never be seduced into the works of the devil. If we have been seduced by Satan already, again, we must repent, renounce it and claim Jesus as our Deliverer and Savior.

CHAPTER 16

LOVE LIFTED ME

It was the power and the authority of the Almighty God that pulled me out of that horrible, dark pit that I was in and broke the iron chains that held me a prisoner. However, it has been the preciousness of the Holy Spirit and the love of Jesus that nourished, enlightened, and lifted me. I will never forget the gentle Holy Spirit breathing on me when I became tired and feeble. That was more powerful than all that Satan could offer.

God's grace was truly sufficient. And often I find myself singing my testimony from that familiar song:

"I was sinking deep in sin, far from the peaceful shore. Very deeply stained within, sinking to rise no more. But the Master of the sea heard my despairing cry, From the waters lifted me now safe am I.

Love lifted me, Love lifted me. When nothing else could help, Love lifted me. Love lifted me, Love lifted me. When nothing else could help, Love lifted me."

Not only has God reached down and taken me out of the darkness to sit with Him in heavenly places, He has restored to me the great blessings of walking in the

---

"Love Lifted Me" by Howard E. Smith, John Benson Publisher, ®
1940.

Light. Even as God promised through Joel (Chap. 2:25, 26) that He would "restore unto you the years that the locust hath eaten, the cankerworm and the caterpillar and the palmerworm, my great army which I sent among you. And ye shall eat in plenty and be satisfied, and praise the Name of the Lord your God, that dealt wondrously with you: and my people shall never be ashamed."

Such has God dealt with me. From the time I was three years old, I could never love a man. Three marriages went from bad to terrible and all failed. After all this, God restored me first as His child and then as a woman. And now He has given me a husband and a father—a man who is a kind, warm, and Spirit-filled Christian.

Admittedly, at first when God brought me to this man, I was very afraid. I was scared that this marriage would be just the same as all the others. But the Holy Spirit reassured me that I had never been free to love before. In fact, I wasn't even me before. Now I was free for the first time to open up to love and receive the love and strength of a man. A new sense of peace, fulfillment and inner confidence that I never knew before has been the result.

I used to lead a coven of dozens but I was really always alone. God has taken away the loneliness that I can now lie down satisfied in plenty. With my husband, I've gained four beautiful children along with a son-in-law and daughters-in-law and eight precious grandchildren. All of these are serving the Lord and two are involved in full-time Christian service for God. All that I was searching for in life is fulfilled in Christ Jesus and walking in His ways. It has not come by my striving—but by His gift of grace.

God is also doing a mighty work of restoration in the lives of my own children. Even as I was a bad example of rebellion, evil and perversion to them for many years, they have seen for six years now a new example of life, joy, freedom and righteousness which they cannot deny. Richard, my son, has seen this way and accepted it as his own, accepting Christ and claiming a new life in Him.

Hope and Peter are now on the fence, acknowledging the reality of God and His miracles in my life, but struggling to find their own identity walking in a world that has been made very confusing by my past life. I have every confidence, however, that God, the Author and Finisher of our faith, will wholly save them according to His promise in Acts 16:31: "Believe on the Lord Jesus Christ and thou will be saved and thy house."

If this book has touched your situation and brought God's light to your life, I want you to know that Jesus Christ will also meet you right where you are with His love. If God could save Irene—and thank God, He has for all eternity—He will save you no matter what you've done or been. Simply come to Him now: ask Him to forgive your sin and come into your life and be your Lord and Spirit Guide (as He now is for me).

God will forgive and cleanse. His power is the greatest. Trust Him and you will stand tall and never again walk in darkness!